How To Lose Your Keys And Find Yourself

Poems for the Beautifully Flawed

Chaitanya S G

BookLeaf
Publishing

India | USA | UK

Made with ❤ on the BookLeaf Publishing Platform
www.bookleafpub.in
www.bookleafpub.com

Dedication

To all the beautifully flawed, the gloriously imperfect, and the wonderfully human: This book is for you.

For the ones who burn toast, lose keys, and spill coffee on their favorite shirt. For the ones who laugh at their own clumsiness and find joy in the chaos. For the overthinkers, the daydreamers, and the ones who cry at dog videos. For those who wear mismatched socks, forget their own birthdays, and still manage to show up —even if they're late.

You are the ones who turn mundane moments into magic, who find meaning in the mess, and who remind us that life isn't about being perfect—it's about being present. Your quirks are your superpowers, your mistakes are your stories, and your flaws are what make you unforgettable.

This book of poems is a love letter to your resilience, your humor, and your ability to find light even on the darkest days. It's a reminder that you're not alone in your awkwardness, your doubts, or your search for meaning. You are enough, just as you are—scuffed edges, crooked smiles, and all.

So here's to you, the beautifully flawed. May you always
find laughter in the little things and poetry in the
everyday.

With love,
Chaitanya S.G

Preface

Life is messy. It's chaotic, unpredictable, and often downright absurd. We lose our keys, burn our toast, and spill coffee on the one clean shirt we own. We overthink, oversleep, and occasionally overheat the microwave. And yet, somehow, in the midst of all this glorious imperfection, we find moments of meaning, connection, and even joy.

This book is a celebration of that messiness. It's a love letter to the beautifully flawed, the wonderfully human, and the gloriously imperfect. Through these acrostic poems, we'll explore the everyday moments that make up our lives—the mundane, the ridiculous, and the unexpectedly profound. From the existential crisis of a jammed printer to the quiet epiphany of a midnight snack, these poems are here to remind you that life's beauty lies not in its perfection, but in its imperfection.

Why acrostics, you ask? Because life, much like poetry, is about finding hidden patterns in the chaos. The acrostic form forces us to look for meaning in the details, just as we search for ourselves in the messiness of daily life. Each poem is a playful puzzle, where the first letters of the lines in the first paragraph spell out a word or phrase that ties into the theme. It's a reminder that even in the most ordinary moments, there's something extraordinary to be found.

As you read these poems, I hope you laugh, nod in recognition, and maybe even shed a tear or two. But most of all, I hope you see yourself in these words. Whether you're a chronic overthinker, a hopeless romantic, or just someone trying to figure out how to adult without setting off the smoke alarm, this book is for you.

So, here's to the beautifully flawed. Here's to the ones who stumble, fall, and get back up again. Here's to finding poetry in the everyday and laughter in the absurd. And here's to you, dear reader, for being exactly who you are—perfectly imperfect, and utterly unforgettable.

Welcome to the journey.

Chaitanya S G

Acknowledgements

To my dearest wife, Manasa, and my precious daughter, Aadhya,

This book would not exist without your unwavering love, patience, and understanding. To say that I am grateful would be an understatement. Manasa, you have been my rock, my confidante, and my greatest supporter, even when my work and writing consumed hours that should have been yours. Your ability to bear with my absences, both physical and mental, is a testament to your strength and love. You've held our world together while I chased words and ideas, and for that, I am forever indebted.

Aadhya, my little star, your laughter and curiosity remind me daily of what truly matters. I know there were times when I was too busy to play, too distracted to listen, or too tired to be fully present. Yet, your unconditional love and bright smile always brought me back to what's important. You are my inspiration, and I hope one day you'll understand why Pappa spent so much time with his books and poems.

To both of you, thank you for bearing with me through the late nights, the missed dinners, and the endless preoccupation. This book is as much yours as it is mine.

With all my love,
Chaitanya.S.G

1. Awaken, You Glorious Mess

Awaken, they say, to a brand-new day,
Like it's a gift, not a debt to pay.
Alarm screams loud, a banshee's cry,
Ripping me from dreams where I could fly.
Must I rise? Must I comply?

Or can I just hit snooze and say, "Goodbye"?
But wait—what if the alarm's not a foe,
But a tiny philosopher, shouting, "Go!"
What if its blaring, its shrill, its beep,
Is life's way of saying, "Wake up, don't sleep!"

For dreams are sweet, but they're not the end,
They're the map, not the journey, my friend.
The bed is cozy, a siren's embrace,
But life's not lived in a pillowcase.

So rise, dear soul, though the world feels absurd,

Though your hair's a nest, though you've forgotten your
words.
For the alarm, in its obnoxious way,
Is a call to adventure, not just to the day.

It's saying, "Get up, you glorious mess,
The world needs your chaos, your laugh, your finesse.
The toaster may jam, the coffee may spill,
But that's where the magic lies—in the imperfect thrill."

So here's to the alarm, that relentless bard,
A wake-up call for the beautifully scarred.
For life's not about getting it right,
It's about showing up, day after night.

2. Brewed Philosophy

Caffeine whispers, "You'll survive,"
Opening my eyes, I feel alive.
Forgive the spills, the stains, the mess,
For coffee's a lifeline, I confess.
Each sip a promise, a brand-new start,
Even with a jittery, caffeinated heart.

But what is coffee, if not a metaphor?
A dark, rich brew of so much more.

It's the warmth of mornings, the buzz of dreams,
The liquid courage in life's wild schemes.
It's the pause in chaos, the calm in the storm,
A ritual of comfort, a daily transform.

From bean to cup, it's a journey of fire,
A reminder that beauty comes from desire.
So here's to the coffee, that magical brew,
A companion in chaos, a friend so true.

For life, like coffee, is bitter and sweet,
A blend of the messy, the wild, the complete.

3. The Toast of Life

The toaster hums, a morning hymn,
Offering hope, though the odds are slim.
A slice of bread, so plain, so meek,
Suddenly transformed, golden and sleek.
Triumph or tragedy? It's hard to say,

For toast, like life, can go either way.
But what is toast, if not a metaphor?
A crispy canvas for so much more.

It's the risk of burning, the joy of perfection,
The art of patience, the need for direction.
It's the butter that melts, the jam that spreads,
The crumbs that fall like tiny threads.

It's the breakfast of champions, the snack of despair,
A reminder that life's not always fair.
So here's to the toast, that humble delight,
A beacon of hope in the morning light.

For life, like toast, is a delicate dance,
A balance of timing, of heat, of chance.

6

4. Lost Keys, Found Self

Keys vanish, as if by design,
Every time I'm running behind.
Yet in the search, I find my way,
Slowly learning to seize the day.

For keys, like life, are prone to stray,
They hide in pockets, in couches, in trays.
They slip through fingers and test our might,
But in the losing, we find the light.

What are keys, if not a riddle to solve?
A tiny rebellion, a playful revolve.
They're the questions we ask when we're running late,
The doors we unlock, the twists of fate.

So here's to the keys, both lost and found,
To the chaos they bring, the peace they've crowned.
For life's not about having it all,
But laughing each time we stumble and fall.

The jingle of metal, the clink of a ring,
Reminds me that joy's in the simplest things.
So next time I'm late, I'll just take a breath,
And laugh at the journey and not fear the depth.

5. Lather, Rinse, Reflect

Steam rises, a morning embrace,
Hot water dreams, a tranquil space.
Oh, but wait—what's this I feel?
Winter's wrath, a frosty ordeal!
Every hope of warmth now dashed,
Replaced by shivers, my calm is trashed.

But what's a shower, if not a test?
A dance of extremes, a liquid quest.
One moment you're basking in tropical bliss,
The next, you're screaming, "What is this?!"

For showers, like life, are full of surprise,
A scalding twist, an icy demise.
They teach us to adapt, to laugh, to endure,
To find joy in the chaos, to stay impure.

What's purity, anyway, but a myth?
A bar of soap, a slippery gift.
We scrub, we rinse, we lather and pray,

But life's messiness never washes away.

And yet, in the steam, there's a moment of grace,
A fleeting escape, a sacred space.
The water may falter, the temperature swing,
But in the shower, we find our thing.

So here's to the showers, both hot and cold,
To the stories they tell, the truths they hold.
For life, like a shower, is a wild ride,
A splash of the silly, a wave of pride.

So next time you're frozen or burned at the start,
Remember: it's art, it's life, it's heart.
And laugh as you lather, and sing as you rinse,
For showers, like life, are a cosmic wince.

6. Reflections of the Soul

My reflection stares, a silent twin,
In a world where outside turns in.
Reversed and yet so much the same,
Reality's echo, a mirrored frame.
Oh, what secrets do you hold,
Reflecting truths both brave and bold?

Step closer, dear reader, and dare to see,
The world inside, where all is free.
A realm where left is right, and right is wrong,
Where silence reigns, yet hums a song.

The mirror's surface, a fragile veil,
A gateway to a parallel tale.
Here, time flows backward, and shadows gleam,
And nothing is quite as it may seem.

What is a mirror, if not a door?
To a world we've known, yet still explore.
It shows us ourselves, yet hides the core,

A paradox we can't ignore.

In this reversed realm, the sky is below,
And rivers of glass in silver flow.
The trees grow downward, their roots in the air,
And laughter is silent, yet everywhere.

But look closer still, and you might find,
A truth that's been hidden, a truth unconfined.
For the mirror reflects not just what's outside,
But the depths of the soul, where truths reside.

So here's to the mirror, that mystical guide,
To the world within, where secrets hide.
For in its reflection, we come to see,
Not just who we are, but who we might be.

7. Threads of Resilience

Silent hero of the shoe's dark abyss,
Often ignored, yet you persist.
Complained about for being smelly,
Knowing full well it's not your belly.

Oh, sock, you bear the brunt of feet,
A sweaty fate, a smelly feat.
You cushion steps, you soak up strife,
Yet rarely thanked in daily life.

And then there's haste, that cruellest foe,
When humans rush, and socks don't show.
One striped, one plain, mismatched pair,
A fashion crime, but do they care?

No, they sprint out, oblivious, blind,
Leaving you, dear sock, behind.
But still, you serve, you stretch, you cling,
Through every step, through everything.

Yet time is cruel, as time will be,
Your fibres fray, your elasticity flees.
You sag, you droop, you lose your grip,
A shadow of your former zip.

And then one day, you're cast aside,
No longer fit for the morning stride.
But here's the truth, dear sock, my friend,
Your worth is more than just an end.

For in your threads, a tale is spun,
Of miles walked, of races run.
Of laughter shared, of journeys made,
Of memories stitched in every grade.

So here's to the sock, that humble mate,
Who bears the stench, who shares the weight.
For though you sag, though you may fray,
You've walked with us, come what may.

8. The Messy Truth

Sudden chaos, a moment's slip,
Pouring coffee, a caffeinated drip.
Ink on paper, a writer's despair,
Leaving behind a smudgy affair.
Life's little spills, both big and small,
Remind us we're human, after all.

The milk spill on the kitchen floor,
A puddle of regret by the fridge door.
But spills aren't just personal, oh no,
They scale up high, they steal the show.

The oil spill in the ocean's embrace,
A global disaster, a tragic case.
The wine spill on a wedding gown,
Turning joy into a teary frown.

Yet here's the truth, dear friend, take heed,
A spill's not the end, it's just a seed.
For every mess, there's a way to mend,

A lesson to learn, a trend to bend.

So when the coffee stains your shirt anew,
Or ink ruins the page you thought you knew,
When milk pools on the kitchen floor,
Or oil blackens the ocean's shore,
Remember this: spills come and go,
But life flows on, and we still grow.

For spills, though messy, teach us grace,
To laugh, to clean, to find our place.
So here's to the spills, both big and small,
For they remind us we can handle it all.

9. Whoopsie Moments

Oh no, I did it again,
Open mouth, insert foot, my friend.
Pouring salt instead of sugar in tea,
Such a classic "oops" moment, you see.

Oh, the "oops" that pepper our days,
The slips, the trips, the clumsy ways.
The text sent to the wrong person's thread,
The buttered toast that lands butter-side down instead.

The "oops" of forgetting a name mid-speech,
The "oops" of wearing pants inside-out to the beach.
The "oops" of spilling wine on the host's white rug,
The "oops" of giving your dog a too-tight hug.

But "oops" isn't just for the small and slight,
It scales up high, it takes flight.
The "oops" of sending an email too soon,
The "oops" of singing off-key at a tune.

The "oops" of burning the dinner to ash,
The "oops" of losing all your cash.
The "oops" of tripping in a crowded place,
The "oops" of smudging mascara all over your face.

Yet here's the truth, dear friend, take note,
An "oops" isn't the end, it's just a anecdote.
For every blunder, there's a story to tell,
A moment of laughter, a tale that swells.

So when you spill, when you slip, when you fall,
Remember, it's not the end of it all.
For "oops" is the spice that flavours our days,
A reminder to laugh at life's quirky ways.

So here's to the "oops," the blunder, the flop,
To the moments that make us laugh nonstop.
For life's not perfect, and that's the charm,
An "oops" is just life's way to disarm.

10. Rise and Reclaim

Ragged breaths, a weary soul,
In the darkness, you feel the toll.
Stumbles and falls, the path is steep,
Even so, you must not sleep.

For in the shadows, a spark remains,
A flicker of hope through all the pains.
It whispers softly, "You are enough,"
A quiet strength, a gentle rebuff.

Rise, dear heart, though the night is long,
Rise, though the world feels cruel and wrong.
Rise, for the dawn is just ahead,
Rise, for the living, not the dead.

You've carried burdens, you've borne the weight,
You've faced the storms, you've met your fate.
But here's the truth, as old as time,
The darkest hour precedes the climb.

So rise, not just to stand, but to fight,
To chase the stars through the endless night.
Rise, not for glory, but for the chance,
To dance again, to dream, to dance.

For every scar, for every tear,
For every moment drowned in fear,
There's a strength within, a fire untamed,
A spirit that cannot be named.

So rise, though the world may doubt,
Rise, though the voices scream and shout.
Rise, for the journey is yours to claim,
Rise, for the world will know your name.

And when you stand, tall and true,
Remember the battles you fought to get through.
For in the rising, you'll come to see,
The greatest victory is to simply be.

11. The Daily Grind

Crawling cars, a sea of steel,
Oh, the traffic, surreal it feels.
Morning madness, horns that blare,
My patience hangs by a threadbare.
Under the sun, or rain, or snow,
This daily grind is a relentless show.
Everyone's racing, but no one's fast,
A symphony of chaos, from first to last.

The bus is packed, the train's delayed,
A stranger's elbow in my ribs has stayed.
The GPS lies, "Just 10 minutes more!"
While I'm stuck in gridlock, my patience sore.

But here's the truth, amidst the strife,
This commute is a metaphor for life.
It's not about speed, or who gets there first,
It's about the journey, quench your thirst.

For in this chaos, there's beauty to find,

A moment to breathe, to clear your mind.
So laugh at the honks, the delays, the fuss,
For life, like traffic, is waiting for us.

So here's to the commute, the daily grind,
A test of patience, a state of mind.
Remember, dear traveler, as you endure,
The journey's the thing, not just the tour.

12. Echoes from the Outbox

Every message begins in the silent theatre of the mind,
Mapping words like battle plans, carefully aligned.
Arranging emotions behind polished prose and grace,
In our heads we rehearse, review, rephrase.
Launch it too fast—and you've already lost the race.

The cursor blinks like a ticking bomb,
While coffee goes cold and fingers drum.
A subject line too vague or bold,
Can start a war or leave hearts cold.

Attachments forgotten, typos bold,
A "Dear Sir" sent to Auntie Gold.
The horror dawns when "Reply All"
Turns private rants into a public brawl.

You click "Send" with shaky breath—
It's done, delivered, doomed or blessed.
But remember this, before you mail:
A word once shot will never trail

Back to its bow—it strikes its mark,
Like arrows loosed through twilight dark.

So take your time and let it rest,
Let calmness craft your clever best.
Emails, like karma, don't forgive haste—
And patience, my friend, is never a waste.

13. A Ring Through the Time

Pigeons carried letters, horses ran miles,
How did we survive without modern wiles?
Oh, the olden days, so slow, so tough,
No instant calls, life was rough.
Every message took weeks to arrive,
A world without phones—how did we thrive?

Then came the phone, a magical thing,
A ring that made the heavens sing.
One phone per street, a shared delight,
Neighbours would gather, day or night.
"Three minutes only!" the operator would say,
As we squeezed our words and saved our pay.

Gradually, phones crept into homes,
A luxury for some, for others, loans.
Rotary dials, cords that stretched,
Conversations that felt truly fetched.
"Can you hear me now?" we'd shout and plead,

A marvel of tech, a growing need.

Then came the mobiles, sleek and small,
Fits in your pocket, answers your call.
From bricks to flip phones, then touchscreens bright,
The world transformed, day and night.
Now everyone's glued, eyes on the screen,
A digital world, where nothing's as it seems.

But here's the twist, the cautionary tale,
This little device can make us frail.
Overuse leads to sleepless nights,
To strained eyes and social plights.
Depression lurks in the endless scroll,
A price we pay for losing control.

So here's to the phone, a revolutionary friend,
But let's not let its power transcend.
Use it wisely, don't let it rule,
Balance is key, don't be its fool.
For life's too rich to live through a screen,
Step back, unplug, and truly be seen.

In laughter and whispers, in eyes that share,
We find the moments that truly declare.
So cherish the phone, as a tool, not a chain,
For love is the message that will always remain.

14. The Glitch in the Matrix

Graphics freeze, the screen turns blue,
Life's little hiccups, we all go through.
In the middle of work, a sudden crash,
Tech reminds us nothing's built to last.
Cursing the code, we restart, reboot,
Hoping the glitch won't take root.

A typo here, a missed cue there,
A glitch in the system, a moment of despair.
The printer jams, the Wi-Fi dies,
The autocorrect fails, and we roll our eyes.
"Why now?" we cry, as the world goes still,
A glitch in the matrix, a bitter pill.

But here's the truth, as old as time,
Glitches are part of life's design.
They teach us patience, they teach us grace,
To laugh at the chaos, to keep up the pace.

For life, like tech, is prone to fail,

A frozen screen, a derailed trail.
But in every glitch, there's a lesson to learn,
A chance to adapt, a chance to discern.

So here's to the glitches, both big and small,
To the moments they humble, the times they appall.
For life's not perfect, and that's the charm,
A glitch is just life's way to disarm.

So next time your world goes haywire,
Remember: glitches can inspire.
They're not the end, just a pause, a hitch,
A reminder to laugh at the occasional glitch.

15. The Beautiful Mess

Children screaming, phones that ring,
Hectic mornings, a chaotic fling.
Appointments missed, the clock's cruel jest,
Organized chaos, we do our best.
Schedules collide, yet somehow, we cope,
Finding beauty in the mess, a sliver of hope.

The kitchen's a war zone, spills on the floor,
The dog's chasing the cat out the door.
Emails pile up, deadlines loom,
The laundry's a mountain, there's no more room.
Yet in this madness, there's a rhythm, a flow,
A dance of chaos that we all know.

For life's not a straight line, neat and clean,
It's a whirlwind of moments, both big and serene.
The traffic jam's rage, the grocery store queue,
The endless to-dos that we power through.
But here's the truth, as wild as it seems,
Chaos is the canvas for our dreams.

Here's to the chaos, the mess, the strife,
The beautiful disorder that shapes our life.
For in every stumble, in every fuss,
There's a lesson to learn, a gift in the muss.

Embrace the chaos, let it swirl and spin,
For it's in the madness that life begins.
We live in organized chaos, it's true,
And somehow, we make it through.

16. The Waking Dream

Drifting through nights, in a world unseen,
Realms of wonder, where nothing's routine.
Every dream a story, a fleeting escape,
Alternate lives in a surreal landscape.
Morning comes, and the visions fade,
But the echoes linger, in light and shade.

Yet dreams aren't confined to the sleep we keep,
They're the hopes we chase, the promises we reap.
The dream of love, the dream of fame,
The dream of success, the dream of a name.

We build our lives on these waking dreams,
Chasing illusions, or so it seems.
But here's the twist, the truth profound,
The real dream is the world around.

For life itself is a dream we share,

A fleeting moment, a breath of air.
The stars, the sky, the earth, the sea,
Are all part of this grand spree.

So wake, dear dreamer, and open your eyes,
The real dream is here, beneath the skies.
For in this dream, there's beauty to find,
In every moment, in every mind.

Let go of the illusions, the false, the scheme,
And embrace the now, the real dream.
For life's not a chase, it's a dance, a stream,
A waking dream, a vibrant theme.

17. The Gift of Rain

Relief whispers in the farmer's prayer,
Asking the skies for a gift so rare.
In the city, the child looks up with hope,
Nature's tears on a dusty slope.

The earth lies parched, cracked and dry,
Under a relentless, burning sky.
The trees stretch high, their leaves turned brown,
The rivers shrink, the wells run down.

The farmer kneels, his hands held high,
"Send us rain, or we'll wither and die."
The child dances, her face to the breeze,
"Please, dear clouds, bring us ease."

And then it comes, a distant roar,
A promise of life, a celestial pour.
The first drop falls, a tender kiss,
A symphony of hope, a moment of bliss.

The rain pours down, a joyful flood,
Quenching the earth, reviving the mud.
The farmer smiles, the child laughs aloud,
The skies have answered, the drought is cowed.

For rain is more than just water's fall,
It's life's renewal, a call to all.
It teaches us patience, it teaches us grace,
To welcome the blessings, no matter the pace.

So here's to the rain, the giver of life,
To the end of struggle, the end of strife.
Let us welcome the rain, let it wash away pain,
For it brings us hope, it brings us life again.

18. Pocket-Sized World

Where dreams and dollars neatly hide,
A tiny vault we keep inside.
Loyal companion, through thick and thin,
Life's little treasures stored within.
Every fold, a story to tell,
The wallet's tale, we know it well.

It holds the cash, the cards, the keys,
The IDs that say, "This is me, please."
A photo tucked in a secret place,
A loved one's smile, a cherished face.
The coins that jingle, a noisy crew,
Pennies and dimes, forgotten but true.

Oh, the wallet, a magical thing,
A pocket-sized world it can bring.
From receipts crumpled, to coupons expired,
To lottery tickets, forever desired.
It's a treasure chest, a time capsule too,
A snapshot of life, both old and new.

But lose your wallet, and chaos ensues,
A frantic search, the dreaded blues.
Cancelled cards, the calls you must make,
The peace of mind, it's quick to break.
For in that wallet, your world resides,
A loss so great, it shakes your insides.

Yet here's the truth, as plain as day,
A wallet's worth is more than pay.
It's a lesson in saving, in spending with care,
In knowing what's precious, what's rare.
For life, like a wallet, is finite, you see,
A balance of giving and keeping the key.

So keep your wallet safe, my friend,
Guard it well, from start to end.
For in its folds, your story's kept,
A life well-lived, a promise well-met.

19. Crunch, Munch, and More

Savory bites, a mood's best friend,
Nibbles that heal, that help us mend.
A treat so small, yet packed with delight,
Crunchy or chewy, a pure respite.
Kids with crumbs, a trail they leave,
Snacking's the joy we all believe.

From fried pakoras, golden and crisp,
To baked cookies, a chocolate kiss.
From raw carrots, a healthy crunch,
To steamed momos, a lunchtime hunch.
The world of snacks is vast and wide,
A universe of taste, with joy inside.

Kids with chips, their hands all greasy,
Giggling loud, their faces easy.
A cookie crumb here, a popcorn trail,
Their snack-time adventures never fail.
For snacks are more than just a bite,

They're moments of joy, pure and bright.

But behind each snack, there's science at play,
From ancient recipes to modern-day.
The chemistry of heat, the art of spice,
The perfect blend, the precise slice.
From grandma's kitchen to labs so sleek,
Snacks are a craft, both old and unique.

Yet here's the truth, as plain as day,
Too much snacking can lead astray.
For life, like snacks, needs balance, you see,
A mix of indulgence and modesty.
So snack with joy, but snack with care,
For health and happiness are a pair.

So here's to the snacks, the treats we adore,
The little delights we can't ignore.
But remember, dear friend, as you munch away,
Eat right, don't snack too much, they say.

20. Eyes on the Prize

Fix your gaze on the path ahead,
Overcome the noise, the doubts you've bred.
Clear your mind, let distractions fade,
Unwavering vision, the plans you've laid.
Steady your heart, and you'll find your way,
Focus is the key to seize the day.

From the camera's lens, sharp and precise,
To the mind's resolve, a priceless device.
Focus in art, in work, in play,
A guiding light that won't betray.
It's the athlete's aim, the writer's flow,
The gardener's patience, the river's glow.

Yet focus is fragile, a fleeting flame,
Distractions whisper, they call your name.
The phone buzzes loud, the world spins fast,
Lose your focus, and the moment's past.
For without it, dreams drift astray,
A ship without sails, lost in the fray.

But here's the truth, as old as time,
Focus is the bridge to the sublime.
It's the warrior's strength, the thinker's might,
The beacon that cuts through the darkest night.
With focus, you conquer, with focus, you rise,
It's the secret behind every prize.

So train your mind, like a muscle, to hold,
To block out the chaos, to be bold.
Set your goals, and keep them near,
Let focus be your guide, your compass, your spear.
For life's battles are won by those who stay true,
Who focus their efforts, who see it through.

So here's to the power of a focused mind,
To the dreams it captures, the treasures it finds.
Have focus, dear friend, and you'll surely succeed,
For it's in the stillness that you'll find the speed.

21. The Silent Healer

Softly now, the day is through,
Lay your burdens, bid adieu.
Every heartbeat, calm and slow,
Eases into dreams that glow.
Peace awaits, in slumber deep,
Sleep, dear soul, and awaken afresh to keep.

From restless nights where shadows creep,
To blissful hours where silence seeps.
Sleep comes in forms, both dark and light,
A fleeting haven, a break from the fight.
The toss and turn, the mind's cruel game,
Or the gentle rest where hearts reclaim.

For sleep is life's great equalizer,
A bridge to dreams, a tranquilizer.
It's the child's nap, the elder's rest,
The worker's pause, the poet's quest.
In sleep, we heal, in sleep, we mend,
A quiet force, a faithful friend.

Yet lose your sleep, and chaos reigns,
A mind unhinged, a soul in chains.
The world grows sharp, the edges cut,
Without sleep's grace, the heart stays shut.
For sleep's not just a pause, a break,
It's the foundation of all we make.

And here's the truth, as old as time,
Sleep is a rhythm, a sacred chime.
Like death, it's a passage, a quiet release,
Like birth, it's a promise, a return to peace.
For every night, we die a little, they say,
And every morning, we're born anew to the day.

So sleep, dear friend, and let go of the strife,
For sleep is the essence of a well-lived life.
It's the pause that refreshes, the calm in the storm,
The cocoon that transforms, the norm to reform.

Sleep to awaken, sleep to rise,
Sleep to see life with fresh, clear eyes.
For in the stillness of night's embrace,
We find the strength to run our race.

So close your eyes, let the world fade away,
For tomorrow's a gift, a brand-new day.

Sleep, dear soul, and awaken afresh,
For sleep is the end, and sleep is the fresh.

44

22. I Am the Shadow, You Are the Flame

Silent mimic, dark and sly,
Haunting every step that I try.
Always there, yet never alone,
Dependent on light to be shown.
Oh foolish pride! To think you're free—
When without Light, you cease to be.

I watched my shadow stand so tall,
Proud and bold against the wall.
"I am myself!" it dared declare,
A form so sharp, a presence rare.
But when the lantern dimmed its glow,
My shadow vanished—where did it go?

The moon then whispered, soft and wise:
"Child of dust, lift your eyes.
You dance and boast, you strut and crow,
But like your shadow, you don't know—
Without the One who gives you form,

You're but a wisp in life's brief storm."

I touched my chest where breath takes flight,
And saw the truth in sudden sight:
My beating heart, this borrowed air,
Are lent by Love beyond compare.
What foolish pride to claim "I AM"
When I'm just shadow—God the Flame.

So let me be what I was made:
A fleeting dance of light and shade.
Not master, but a mirror true,
Reflecting Glory not my due.
For shadows teach what sages know—
We're nothing till His light we show.

23. When Nothing Married Everything

Softly, the Void whispered to the All,
In a language beyond time's wall.
Like shy lovers meeting at twilight's crest,
Everything blushed, and Nothing was dressed
Not in stars, nor in space—just a sigh—
Cradling the birth of the first "Why?"
Eternity paused... then winked its reply.

Oh, how Nothing courted the Everything!
With no gifts but the songs it would sing—
No clocks to tick, no maps to guide,
Just Silence dancing with cosmic pride.
"Shall we?" asked the All to the Naught,
And the universe sparked from the kiss they wrought.

From their embrace burst Something new—
A giggle of quarks, a sky of blue,
Oceans swirling, mountains tall,
All because Silence said, "Let there be All!"

Yet deep in the core of each newborn sun,
The lovers still hum their ageless tune.

We children of Something, so loud, so bold,
Forgot how Silence cradles the world.
We chase the noise, the rush, the more,
While the primal hush knocks at our door:
"Come home," it calls, "to where you began—
The space between notes where God first sang."

So let us return, just you and I,
To the love song of Earth and Sky.
For in the pause, in the breath, in the gap,
We meet the ones who first said it all..."

24. Two Compasses: A Seeker's Anthem

Shivering hands scrawl shopping lists in gold,
Earthly treasures bought and sold.
Across the world, the hungry roam—
Rich or poor, no one stays home.
Chasing tails in endless spins,
How loud the search for things begins!

Yet deeper stirs a second cry,
A whisper even kings deny:
"Who lights this lamp behind my eyes?
What breathes my breath? What dreams my skies?"
No market sells this sacred thread,
No map leads where the soul is led.

The scholar digs through dusty books,
The monk in caves divines his looks,
The lover seeks in arms of clay,
Yet still the Question burns away:
"Am I the wave, or am I sea?

Or just a thought that thinks 'I'm me'?"

Oh restless heart! Don't you see?
The search itself is homecoming's key.
Not in answers—but in kneeling low,
Where winds of why still blow.
Keep that inner lantern bright,
Though shadows dance with stolen light.

For all the world's a fleeting show,
But what watches—that will know.
So search, dear fool, both far and wide,
Then turn the compass deep inside.
The day you stop—that's when you'll find
The seeker and sought were never twined.

25. The Gravity of Grins

Storms may tear your sails apart,
Mock your maps, yet—soft your heart.
In the wreckage, choose to glow,
Like dawn insists through midnight's woe.
Every grin forges armor bright,
Melting shadows into light.

When crops wither, when coins flee,
When doors slam where keys should be,
When the body aches and bends,
When you lose yet still defend—
That's when smiles wield sacred power,
Turning bitter hours sweet and sour.

Not the smirk of fools who blind
Themselves to pain—but souls refined
By fires no eyes will ever see,
Yet still choose gentle gravity.
A smile that knows the weight of stone
But lifts it, though it stands alone.

Work? Oh yes, dig deep and sweat,
Let your hands stay scarred and wet.
Persistence carves through mountains tall,
But hear this truth above it all:
No triumph tastes its sweetest bloom
Till smiled upon through grief and gloom.

For life's no ledger, cold and fair,
But breath we shape from common air.
The grin that greets what fate may bring
Is the bravest act of worshipping.
So wear your joy like warriors do—
Not for luck, but because it's true.

When last light fades, when all seems vain,
Remember: Smiles are sovereign rain
That nourish seeds where failures fell.
What blooms tomorrow? None can tell.
But today? Today you chose to shine—
The oldest magic, wholly thine.

26. Tongues of Flame, Hands of Reign

Dancing flames that lick the sky,
Embers whispering "Reach! Aspire!"
Searing hunger, sweet and dire,
In my ribs, a furnace glows—
Racing steeds no rider knows,
Each one lunging for their fire.

See my chariot—gilded, bright,
Five wild horses charge the night:
One for pleasure, one for gold,
One for stories never told,
One for power cruel and bold,
One that screams "More!" in my ear—
How their nostrils flare with fear!

Oft they've dragged me through the dirt,
Snapping reins with reckless hurt,
Burning huts where children slept,
While my weeping vigil kept.

Now I learn what sages say:
"Steeds must serve, not lead the way."

With woven threads of will I stand,
Not to kill, but to command.
Let them run—but run through me,
Harnessed flames that set me free.
For desire's neither friend nor foe,
But sacred oil that makes souls grow.

27. Ceasefire: A Soul's White Flag

Pale happiness comes and goes,
Echoing laughter, fading rose.
Ah, but peace—still as the deep,
Calm no storm can touch or keep.
Endless sky where tempests cease—
This is the kingdom called true peace.

See how nations raise their guns,
"Fighting for peace" beneath dead suns.
Tanks that roll through children's parks,
Freedom's scream in concrete arcs.
The soul too wars with mirrored might—
Fear and love clash through the night.

Happiness? A fickle tide,
Wine that sparkles, then dries inside.
It dances on your palm awhile,
Then flees like April's teasing smile.
But peace remains when joys depart,

The steady drum within your heart.

No treaty signed in blood-stained halls,
No vaults of gold or fortress walls
Can gift what comes when fighting ends—
When the warrior within transcends.
For peace isn't land your flags decree,
But the space where you let all things be.

So plant your feet on this sacred ground
Where silence blooms without a sound.
Let happiness flirt, beguile, deceive—
Peace is knowing you needn't grieve.
The bombs may fall, the world may shake,
But here, in this, no one can take:

The still small voice that needs no proof,
The ocean floor beneath life's roof.
Come home, fierce soul, lay down your sword,
Peace was never won—it's remembered, Lord.

28. Temporary Stains

Crimson dawn births golden beams,
Oh how the prism paints its dreams!
Liquid sapphire, emerald leaves,
One white light the rainbow weaves.
Until the brush of dusk descends low—
Returning all to indigo.

Watch how colours cast their spell:
Red will rage or love compels,
Blue sings truth or drowns in sorrow,
Yellow laughs or warns of morrow.
Even black—the void's disguise—
Holds starlight in its velvet eyes.

Seven hues from one sun born,
A million shades by twilight worn.
Yet grind them down to atoms bare,
Find just light and empty air.
What magic is this? That form appears
Then vanishes beyond the years!

So live your palette, bold and bright,
Drench your days in sheer delight.
When grey clouds cloak your azure skies,
Remember: shadows magnify dyes.
For pain's dark thread, when wisely spun,
Makes joy's gold shine threefold sun.

Fear not the stains of time and fate,
Each smear becomes your sacred slate.
Till one day, when the show is through,
You'll laugh—all colours melt to You.
That radiant white where all began...
Just God playing peekaboo, man.

29. Grace Notes

Gentle hands that first held me tight—
Rock of ages, my mother's right.
A father's nod that said "Go on,"
Courage woven before dawn.
Eternal gifts no gold could trace—
This is the first face of Grace.

Brother's grace in shared old shoes,
Passed-down dreams, their laces loose.
Teacher's grace—that chalk-dust spark,
Turning streetlights into stars.
Master's grace, the sternest kiss:
"Break your heart to find your bliss."

Not luck, nor chance, but Grace alone
Turns stone to milk, makes sandstorms hone.
It lights the poor man's single lamp,
Steadies the drunkard's trembling ramp.
Grace is what remains when "I" decays—
The hand that lifts when pride betrays.

So kneel daily, foolish king,
To dandelions and cricket wings.
Thank the mud where lotuses root,
Thank the boot that bruised your foot.
For Grace flows where gratitude starts,
Through broken doors and mended hearts.

When triumph crowns your sweaty brow,
Or when you're crushed—remember how:
Grace never kept a merchant's book,
It floods where no dams ever look.
Drink it deep, this cosmic wine,
Till "yours" and "mine" blur into Thine

30. Liberation's Final Joke

Loosen first the petty chains—
Idleness that numbs your veins,
Bitterness that sours wine,
Ego's whisper "You are mine."
Rage that burns your sacred ground,
All these shackles must be drowned.
Till you stand naked, raw, and true,
Empty hands facing the blue.

Next, unknot the subtler ties:
Pride in virtue, light that blinds,
Even bliss can be a cage
If you cling to any stage.
Peel the layers, skin the mind,
Leave no footprint to remind.

Now the final crucifix—
Slay the fear of birth's strict fix.
Die before your death arrives,
Watch the corpse of "I" survive

Just long enough to know it's dead,
Then burn the bier where it was laid.

What remains when all is gone?
Not a saint, not a pawn,
But the sky before clouds form,
The silence before the storm,
The Almighty's naked name
That breathes your breath, burns your flame.

Here, no sorrow, no delight,
Only That which has no height.
No more cycles, no return,
Just the Fire that cannot burn.
Liberated? Don't be deceived—
You were never bound, just dreamed.